MISSION CONTROL

THE OSIRIS-REx MISSION

SOPHIE WASHBURNE

PowerKiDS press

Published in 2025 by The Rosen Publishing Group, Inc.
2544 Clinton Street, Buffalo, NY 14224

First Edition

Special thanks to Kristen Baroudi, Ph.D., for providing chemistry consultation.

Editor: Jennifer Lombardo
Book Design: Rachel Rising

Photo Credits: Cover, p. 16 Raymond Cassel/Shutterstock.com; cover, pp. 1, 3–32 KK.KICKIN/Shutterstock.com; p. 4 Triff/Shutterstock.com; p. 5 Lukasz Pawel Szczepanski/Shutterstock.com; p. 6 Nazarii_Neshcherenskyi/Shutterstock.com; p. 7 D1min/Shutterstock.com; p. 8 https://en.m.wikipedia.org/wiki/File:OSIRIS-REx_landing.jpg; pp. 9, 17 NASA/Goddard/University of Arizona; p. 11 xfilephotos/Shutterstock.com; p. 12 Gorodenkoff/Shutterstock.com; p. 13 LeonART Studio/Shutterstock.com; p. 14 Frame Stock Footage/Shutterstock.com; p. 15 Mascha Tace/Shutterstock.com; pp. 17, 22 https://commons.wikimedia.org/wiki/File:OSIRIS-REx_candidate_sample_sites_on_Bennu.png; pp.18, 28 joshimerbin/Shutterstock.com; p. 19 NASA/Erika Blumenfeld & Joseph Aebersold; p. 20 https://en.m.wikipedia.org/wiki/File:OSIRIS-REx_Sample_Return_(NHQ202309240005).jpg; p. 21 https://commons.wikimedia.org/wiki/File:OSIRIS-REx_Sample_Return_(NHQ202309240002).jpg; p. 23 Platon Anton/Shutterstock.com; p. 24 Marko Aliaksandr/Shutterstock.com; p. 25 patrisyu/Shutterstock.com; p. 26 buradaki/Shutterstock.com; p. 27 https://en.m.wikipedia.org/wiki/File:PIA17202_-_Approaching_Enceladus.jpg; p. 29 Jean-Baptiste Toussaint/Shutterstock.com.

Library of Congress Cataloging-in-Publication Data
Names: Washburne, Sophie.
Title: The OSIRIS-REx mission / Sophie Washburne.
Description: Buffalo, NY : PowerKids Press, 2025. | Series: Mission control | Includes glossary and index.
Identifiers: ISBN 9781499449846 (pbk.) | ISBN 9781499449853 (library bound) | ISBN 9781499449860 (ebook)
Subjects: LCSH: OSIRIS-REx Asteroid Sample Return Mission--Juvenile literature. | Space flight to asteroids--Juvenile literature. | Asteroids--Juvenile literature. | Bennu (Asteroid)--Juvenile literature.
Classification: LCC QB651 .W37 2025 | DDC 523.44--dc23

Manufactured in the United States of America

CONTENTS

IN THE BEGINNING 4
UNDERSTANDING ASTEROIDS 6
TO BENNU AND BACK 8
THE MISSION 10
BUILDING OSIRIS-REX 12
LIFTOFF! 14
THE RIGHT SPOT 16
TOUCHDOWN! 18
DROPPING OFF 20
FINDINGS 22
WHAT DOES IT MEAN? 26
OSIRIS-APEX 28
GLOSSARY 30
FOR MORE INFORMATION 31
INDEX 32

IN THE BEGINNING

About 4.6 billion years ago, the gas and dust in a **nebula** began to clump together and form a dense ball. The denser the ball got, the hotter it got. This hot, dense ball began to spin, forming a **protostar**. More and more matter was pulled into the protostar, and it continued to grow hotter and denser. Finally, the protostar was large enough to become a true star—our sun.

About 99 percent of the matter in the nebula was pulled in to create the sun. The remaining 1 percent formed everything else in our solar system. The sun's gravity caused all these objects to start orbiting around it. They range in size from very large planets to very tiny pieces of rock.

Our sun is the largest object in the solar system. More than 1.3 million Earths could fit inside it.

UNDERSTANDING ASTEROIDS

Every bit of matter that did not become part of the sun, planets, or moons when our solar system formed became free-floating **debris**. This includes comets, asteroids, and meteoroids. Scientists believe that when Jupiter formed in the early days of the solar system, the planet was so big that it stopped other planets from forming nearby.

After Jupiter finished forming, objects either got pulled into the planet's orbit to become its moons or pushed away from it quickly. This caused pieces of debris to smash into each other, creating millions of smaller pieces of rock. Each piece is an asteroid. The asteroids fell into orbit around the sun, creating what we know today as the asteroid belt between Mars and Jupiter. This is where most asteroids in the solar system can be found.

WHAT'S THE DIFFERENCE?

Comets, asteroids, and meteoroids are all pieces of debris left over from the beginning of the solar system. Comets are mostly made up of ice and dust. Asteroids are mostly made up of rock and metal. Meteoroids are pieces of rock that are smaller than asteroids. When a meteoroid enters Earth's atmosphere and burns up, we call it a meteor or a shooting star. If a piece of the meteor lands on Earth, we call that piece a meteorite.

This picture shows the location of the asteroid belt.

TO BENNU AND BACK

In 2004, two researchers at the University of Arizona—Michael Drake and Dante Lauretta—began to talk about the possibility of an asteroid sample return mission. This meant a spacecraft would land on an asteroid, collect samples, and bring them back to Earth. It took seven years to convince NASA to run the mission, but finally the agency agreed.

The research team chose a near-Earth asteroid called Bennu for the mission. There were several reasons for this. One was that, as an asteroid that passes close to Earth, Bennu was fairly easy to get to. Researchers also did not have to wait many years for the spacecraft to complete its journey. Furthermore, scientists believed that Bennu could contain organic materials, or materials that are needed to create life.

NASA KNOWLEDGE

Bennu was discovered in 1999 and originally known as 1999 RQ36. In 2013, nine-year-old Mike Puzio from North Carolina won a contest to name the asteroid.

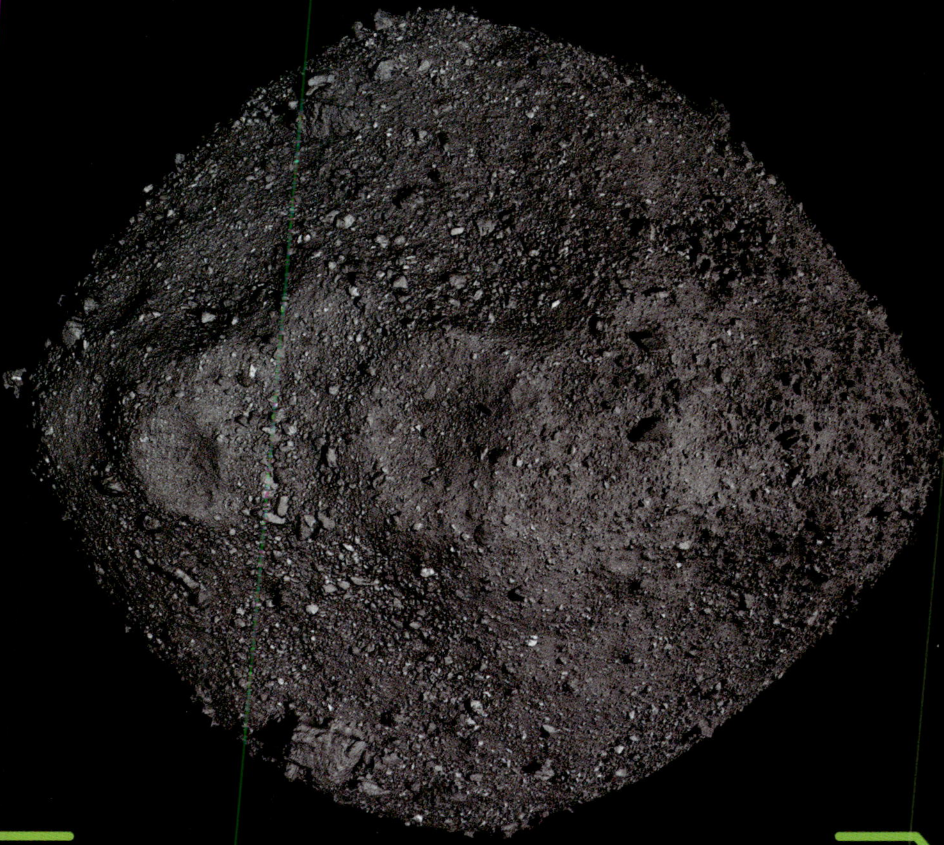

This picture of Bennu was stitched together from multiple different pictures that were taken over the course of two years.

THE MISSION

By going to Bennu, researchers hoped to learn a lot. One thing they wanted to find out was what the solar system was like when it was first forming. On Earth, forces such as weather, erosion, plate tectonics, and human activity have completely changed the planet over time. However, in space, those forces do not exist. Bennu is the same now as it was when it first formed.

Researchers also want to know how life started on Earth. One theory is that asteroids similar to Bennu crashed into the planet when it was still forming and deposited water and organic matter. Comparing samples of Bennu to samples taken from Earth could help scientists learn more about this early part of our history.

NASA KNOWLEDGE

Studying an asteroid may also help answer questions such as, "Can we stop asteroids from hitting Earth?" and "Can asteroids be used as fuel?"

Our planet is constantly changing. This picture shows the process of erosion caused by water.

BUILDING OSIRIS-REx

Once NASA accepted the mission, engineers got to work building the spacecraft that would go to Bennu. They named it Origins, **Spectral** Interpretation, Resource Identification, and Security-**Regolith** Explorer, or OSIRIS-REx. The name includes some of the mission's main goals. To make sure these goals could all be met, engineers had to design the spacecraft very carefully.

To map and study Bennu, the engineers gave the spacecraft instruments, or tools, such as cameras, spectrometers, and a lidar system. Lidar uses a laser to create a detailed map of something—in this case, Bennu's surface. To collect a sample, the engineers created a system where OSIRIS-REx could blow a stream of nitrogen gas onto the asteroid to stir up some of its regolith. Some of that regolith was then caught in a container.

INSPIRED BY MYTHOLOGY

Dante Lauretta and Michael Drake were the two researchers at the University of Arizona who first suggested an asteroid return mission. When Lauretta was trying to figure out a name for the mission based on its goals, he noticed some similarities to the Egyptian god Osiris. According to mythology, Osiris brought knowledge of farming to the world, which made modern life possible. Since asteroids may also have brought life to Earth, Lauretta and Drake agreed that Osiris was a good name for the mission. "REx" was added later.

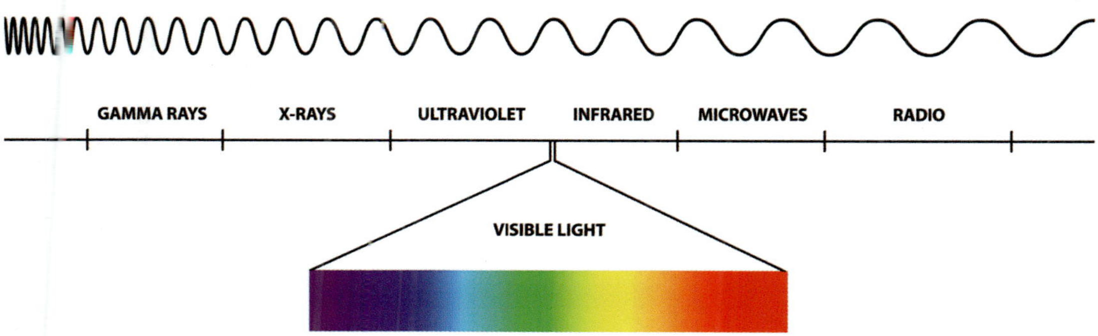

A spectrometer examines an object using different **wavelengths** on the electromagnetic spectrum. OSIRIS-REx has both infrared and x-ray spectrometers.

LIFTOFF!

NASA launched OSIRIS-REx on September 8, 2016. The spacecraft touched down on Bennu on October 20, 2020. It collected its sample and returned to Earth on September 24, 2023. Although this process sounds simple, it took a lot of skill as well as some luck.

While OSIRIS-REx was in space, NASA engineers on the ground had to **monitor** it to make sure it stayed on its trajectory, or path, toward Bennu. The spacecraft had rockets called thrusters that could be turned on to point it in the right direction. It arrived at Bennu on December 3, 2018, and spent the next two years mapping the asteroid's surface and sending photos back to NASA.

GRAVITY ASSIST

NASA scientists used Earth's gravity to help OSIRIS-REx get onto the right trajectory. On September 22, 2017, the spacecraft flew over Antarctica, heading north toward the Pacific Ocean. This helped OSIRIS-REx move out of Earth's **orbital plane** and onto Bennu's, which is six degrees from Earth's. Earth's gravity also acted like a slingshot, flinging OSIRIS-REx out into space and helping it get to Bennu a little bit faster than it otherwise would have.

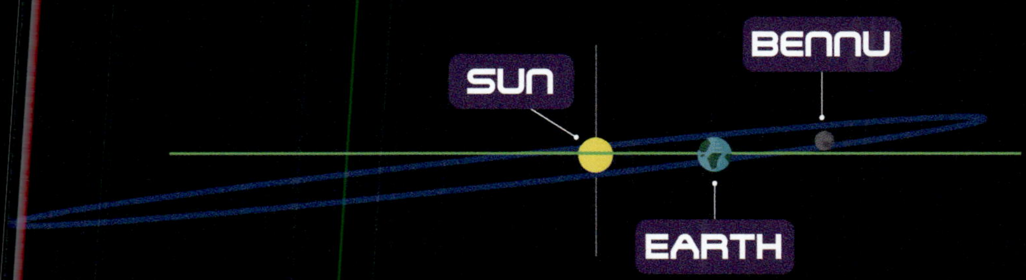

Bennu has a different orbital plane than Earth does. To reach it, OSIRIS-REx had to use Earth's gravity to change its trajectory.

THE RIGHT SPOT

Part of the reason OSIRIS-REx stayed in orbit around Bennu for two years was so NASA could decide on the best place for it to land. Bennu's surface is covered in sharp rocks, and landing the wrong way or in the wrong place could have damaged the spacecraft.

NASA scientists picked out four spots on Bennu that they believed would be the best places for OSIRIS-REx to land. Each one was given a score based on four factors. The first was how safe it would be for OSIRIS-REx to land there. The second was the size of the samples available. To be easily collected in OSIRIS-REx's container, the rocks and dirt could not be larger than 1 inch (2.5 cm) across. The third factor was how easy it would be to get OSIRIS-REx into and out of the site. The fourth was how informative the possible samples could be.

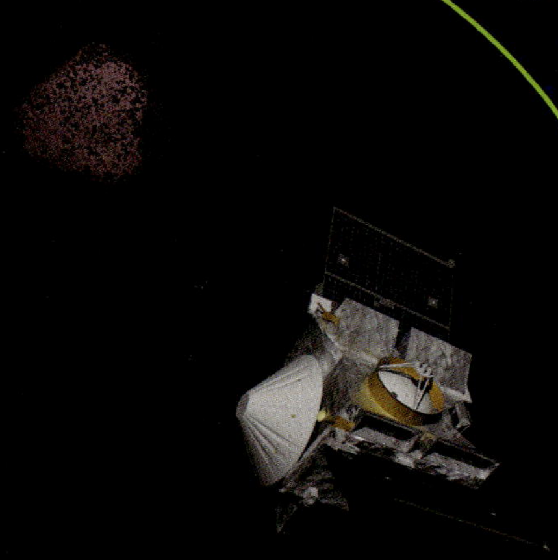

NASA KNOWLEDGE

Each of the four sample sites was named after a bird. They were Site Nightingale, Site Osprey, Site Kingfisher, and Site Sandpiper.

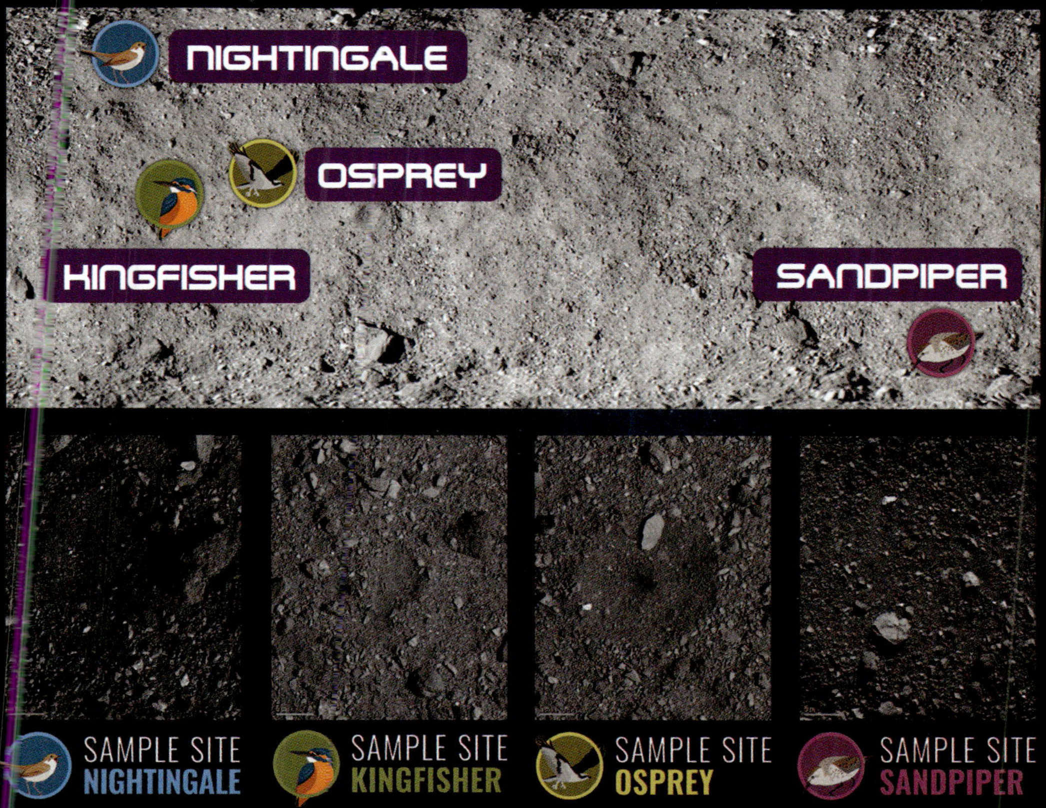

This picture shows the location of each possible landing site.

TOUCHDOWN!

After studying OSIRIS-REx's photos and maps for a year, the team finally chose Site Nightingale as the primary, or main, landing site. It was in a crater about 460 feet (140 meters) wide on the northern end of the asteroid. They chose Site Osprey as a backup, just in case the sample collection could not be completed at Nightingale for some reason.

The backup plan was not needed. Everything went as planned. OSIRIS-REx used an extendable robotic arm to complete a "touch-and-go," or TAG, **maneuver**. This meant the spacecraft never fully landed; it just touched the surface of the asteroid with its arm, collected the 2-ounce (60 g) sample NASA needed, and took off again.

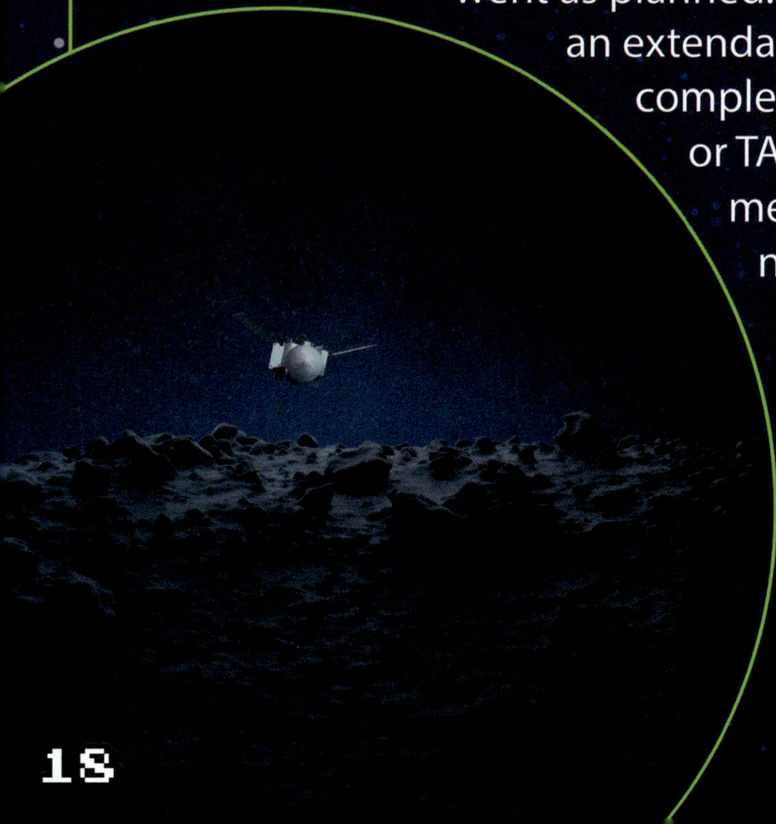

WHY NIGHTINGALE?

Of the four sites, Nightingale had the most loose, small regolith material and the fewest large, sharp rocks. Additionally, the regolith at Site Nightingale was darker than at the other three sites. This led scientists to believe that the crater was newer, which meant the regolith in it would be fairly **uncontaminated**—the closest to the way Bennu was when it first formed.

Some of Bennu's regolith can be seen on the outside of this container. Scientists collected this material along with what was inside. In total, they obtained 4.29 ounces (121.6 g) of material.

DROPPING OFF

After OSIRIS-REx collected its sample, it made the long journey back to our planet. On April 7, 2021, the spacecraft made its last flyover of Bennu and turned toward Earth. On May 10, it fired its thrusters to give it a push in the right direction. OSIRIS-REx orbited the sun twice before reaching Earth. When it was in the right spot, OSIRIS-REx released the capsule, or part, that held the Bennu samples.

After the capsule made it through Earth's atmosphere, it opened a **parachute** that allowed it to float gently down to the ground. On September 24, 2023, the capsule landed in a part of Utah's West Desert that is controlled by the Department of Defense. NASA picked it up from there.

DIVIDING THE SAMPLE

NASA scientists took the sample capsule back to one of its labs, which had been built specifically for the study of the Bennu sample. The University of Arizona led the study, with other members of the team picked from science organizations all over the world. This team was given 25 percent of the sample. The rest was preserved so it can be studied more in the future, when scientists may have even better technology than they do today.

The capsule was blackened by the heat of its passage through Earth's atmosphere.

FINDINGS

As soon as NASA began studying the Bennu sample, scientists learned some amazing things. They found that, as expected, the regolith contained organic material as well as carbon and nitrogen—two elements that were an important part of the solar system's formation. However, they also found several surprises.

Scientists found clay minerals that make the sample very similar to the kind of rock that is found in Earth's oceans, specifically at places where material from the mantle mixes with water. This suggests that the Bennu sample was once covered in water. The sample also contains water-**soluble** compounds that all living creatures need. Scientists were not expecting to find these compounds on Bennu.

After studying the Bennu sample, scientists have some hypotheses, or ideas, about the early days of our solar system.

NASA KNOWLEDGE

The sample capsule was harder to open than NASA had expected. Scientists started opening it in October 2023, but they were unable to take off two of the bolts that kept the container closed. Work was paused while new tools were made, and the container was finally opened in January 2024.

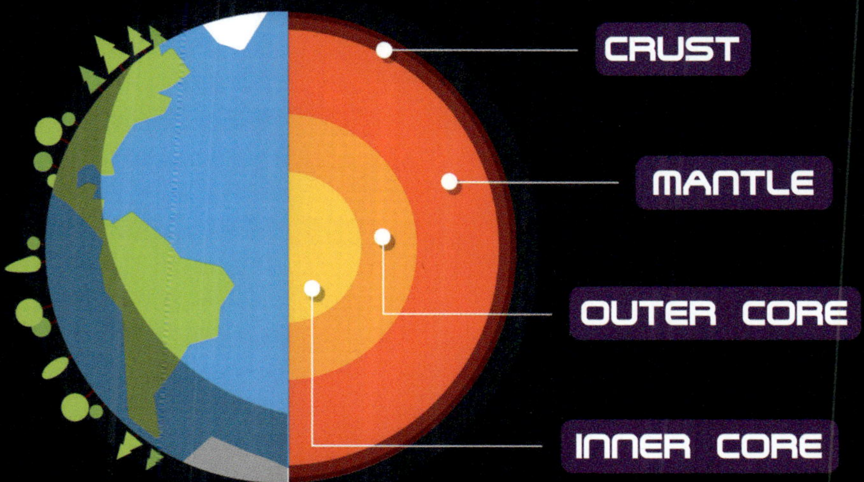

This picture shows the different layers of Earth.

The team also found a mineral in the sample called magnesium-sodium phosphate. This was also unexpected. When the team first found it, they thought the sample might have been contaminated somewhere between Bennu and Earth. However, after further study, they realized that it is part of Bennu's regolith.

The scientists were excited to find this phosphate because they did not realize it was present on Bennu. OSIRIS-REx's instruments didn't detect it when it first scanned the asteroid. It may be present in other asteroids or meteorites, but scientists believe it either burns up when a meteorite enters the atmosphere or disappears after a few days in Earth's air. It was only found because NASA got a sample directly from space and protected it all the way from Bennu to the lab. Scientists hope that by studying the sample further, they can learn more about Bennu's history.

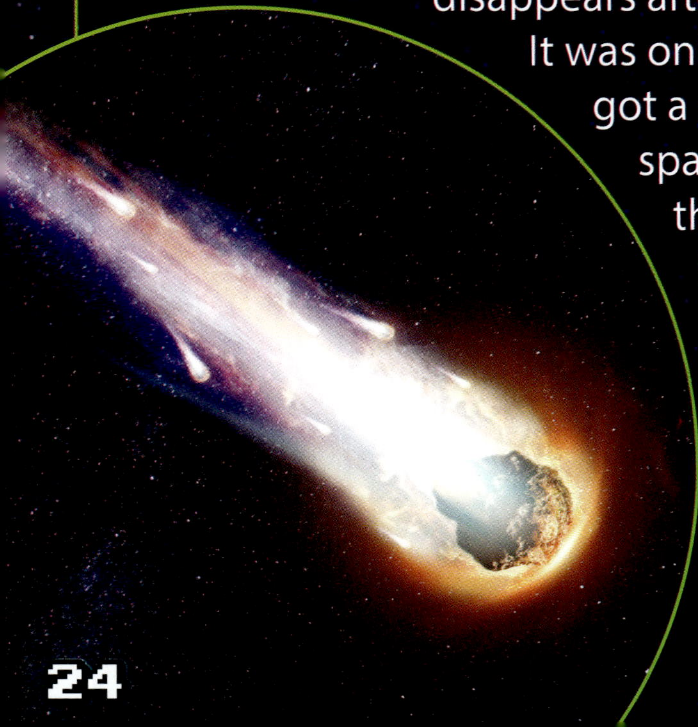

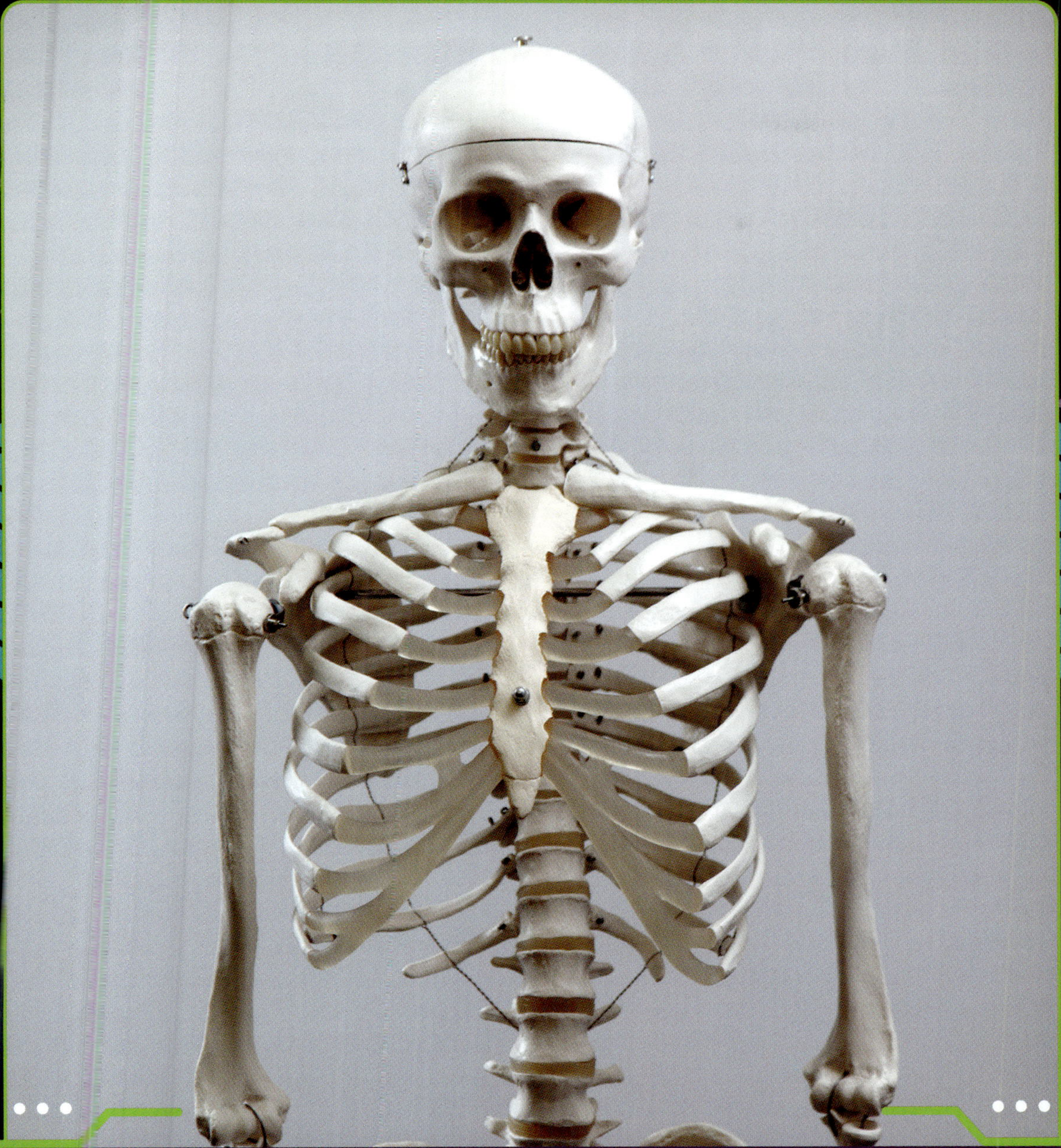

A phosphate is formed when the element phosphorus combines with oxygen. Many different kinds of phosphates can be found on Earth, including some in our bones and teeth.

WHAT DOES IT MEAN?

Much more study is needed before scientists can say anything for sure about the solar system's formation in general and about Bennu's or Earth's history in particular. However, they have some guesses right now, based on what they learned from the sample. The presence of clay minerals and organic material suggests that Bennu was once part of a world that was covered in water.

The magnesium-sodium phosphate backs up this idea because it is water-soluble. Scientists believe it is possible that Bennu is a piece of debris that broke off of a larger planet. Many scientists picture a large, muddy planet that was destroyed about 3 billion years ago by a collision with a much larger object. The collision would have sent pieces like Bennu flying until they were dragged into orbit in the asteroid belt. The water would have evaporated without an atmosphere to hold it in.

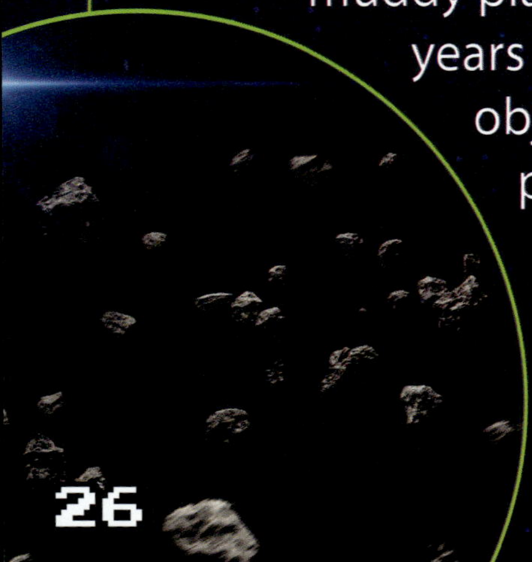

NASA KNOWLEDGE

As of mid-2024, the Bennu team has studied less than 1 percent of the sample. The more they study, the more they will learn.

Studies show that under the ice of Saturn's moon Enceladus is a large, liquid ocean that contains phosphates like the ones found in the Bennu sample. Bennu may once have been part of a world like this.

OSIRIS-APEX

When OSIRIS-REx dropped off the Bennu sample, it didn't land on Earth. It didn't even enter the atmosphere. Instead, it stayed in space, ready to study another asteroid called Apophis. The spacecraft was renamed OSIRIS-APEX, with APEX standing for "Apophis Explorer." Scientists who study asteroids say Apophis's orbit will take it within 20,000 miles (32,000 km) of Earth in 2029.

When Apophis gets close to Earth, OSIRIS-APEX will enter its orbit. It will then take samples and map the asteroid's surface, just as it did with Bennu. Astronomers hope these samples will confirm what they already know as well as give them new information, just as Bennu's sample did. Dr. Daniella Mendoza DellaGiustina a researcher at the University of Arizona, will lead the OSIRIS-APEX team.

Apophis was an Egyptian snake-god who represented destruction. For a while, astronomers thought the asteroid Apophis was likely to hit Earth. Further study showed that this is not the case.

GLOSSARY

debris: The remains of something that has been broken.

maneuver: A planned movement.

monitor: To observe carefully for a period of time.

nebula: A cloud of gas and dust in space.

orbital plane: The geometric plane in which the orbit of a revolving body lies.

parachute: An umbrella-shaped piece of cloth that collects air to slow something down.

protostar: A mass of dust and gas that is in the process of becoming a star.

regolith: Loose pieces of rock and dust that sit on top of a thicker layer of rock.

soluble: Able to be dissolved.

spectral: Having to do with the light spectrum.

uncontaminated: Not ruined by the presence of another material.

wavelength: The distance from crest to crest or trough to trough of a wave.

FOR MORE INFORMATION

BOOKS

Lawrence, Ellen. *Comets, Meteors, and Asteroids: Voyagers of the Solar System*. Chicago, IL: Sequoia Kids Media, 2022.

Mather, Charis. *Asteroids and Comets: Top-Secret Data*. Minneapolis, MN: Bearport Publishing, 2024.

Ventura, Marne. *Asteroids*. Lake Elmo, MN: Focus Readers, 2023.

WEBSITES

BrainPOP: Asteroids
www.brainpop.com/topic/asteroids
Watch a short movie and take a quiz to test your knowledge of asteroids.

NASA: OSIRIS-REx Resources
science.nasa.gov/solar-system/resources/resource-packages/osiris-rex-resources
This page has information as well as fun crafts and activities focused on the OSIRIS-REx mission.

YouTube: How Far Did OSIRIS-REx Plunge Into Asteroid Bennu?
www.youtube.com/watch?v=wCO1y_GNo98
This video from NASA shows an animation of how OSIRIS-REx collected its samples from Bennu.

Publisher's note to educators and parents: Our editors have carefully reviewed these websites to ensure that they are suitable for students. Many websites change frequently, however, and we cannot guarantee that a site's future contents will continue to meet our high standards of quality and educational value. Be advised that students should be closely supervised whenever they access the internet.

INDEX

A
Apophis, 28, 29
asteroid belt, 6, 7, 26
asteroids, 6, 7, 8, 9, 10, 13, 14, 18, 24, 26, 28, 29
atmosphere, 7, 20, 21, 24, 26, 28

B
Bennu, 8, 9, 10, 12, 14, 15, 16, 18, 19, 20, 21, 22, 24, 26, 27, 28

C
cameras, 12
carbon, 22
comets, 6, 7

D
debris, 6, 7, 26
DellaGiustina, Dr. Daniella Mendoza, 28
Drake, Michael, 8, 13
dust, 4, 7

E
erosion, 10, 11

G
gas, 4, 12
gravity, 4, 15

I
ice, 7

J
Jupiter, 6

L
landing sites, 16, 17, 18, 19
Lauretta, Dante, 8, 13
lidar system, 12

M
Mars, 6
metal, 7
meteorite, 7, 24
meteoroids, 6, 7
meteors, 7
moons, 6, 27

N
NASA, 8, 12, 14, 15, 16, 18, 20, 21, 22, 23, 24
nebula, 4
nitrogen, 12, 22

O
orbital plane, 15
organic materials, 8, 10, 22, 26
OSIRIS-APEX, 28

P
phosphates, 24, 25, 26, 27
planets, 4, 6, 26
protostar, 4

R
regolith, 12, 19, 22, 24
rock, 4, 6, 7, 16, 19, 22

S
sample, 8, 10, 12, 14, 16, 17, 18, 20, 21, 22, 23, 24, 26, 27, 28
Saturn, 27
shooting stars, 7
solar system, 4, 5, 6, 7, 10, 22, 26
spectrometers, 12, 13
sun, 4, 5, 6, 10, 20

T
TAG maneuver, 18

U
University of Arizona, 8, 13, 21, 28

W
water, 10, 11, 22, 26